My name's **Microchip** – but you can call me Chip. I might be small, but I'm really important to **technology**.

Because of me, you can play video games, listen to music on an MP3 player, and talk on a mobile phone.

an MP3 player

a mobile phone

Cool Things about Chip

I was **invented** in 1958. Since then, I've come a long way. Thanks to me, **computers** are now small and easy to make.

a microchip

- I hold thousands of **transistors** and **electrical circuits.**
- I'm made from silicon, a material found in sand, clay or stone.
- My parts are so small that one thousand of my wires could fit into one strand of your hair!

Some microchips are so small, even ants are bigger than them!

a microchip

Computer Timeline

Before I was invented, computers were huge and slow. Some early computers were as big as a room! But they had less power than a calculator does today.

3000 BC – the Abacus

The first "computer" was a counting machine. It was called the abacus. You can still use an abacus today.

Excellent Gadgets – Now and Then

Elizabeth Corfe

Contents

Meet Chip

Hello! Can you see me? I'm here on this page, but I'm teeny tiny.

a video game

1822 – Babbage's Machine

A man called Charles Babbage invented this machine to add up! It was never finished. But many people now call Charles Babbage the "father of the computer".

1946 – ENIAC

The first electronic computer was called ENIAC. It was the size of a small house!

1977 – Apple II

The Apple II was a **personal** computer (PC). It had a colour screen and its own keyboard.

2008 – iPhone

An iPhone is a computer and mobile phone in one. You can use it to make phone calls and surf the internet.

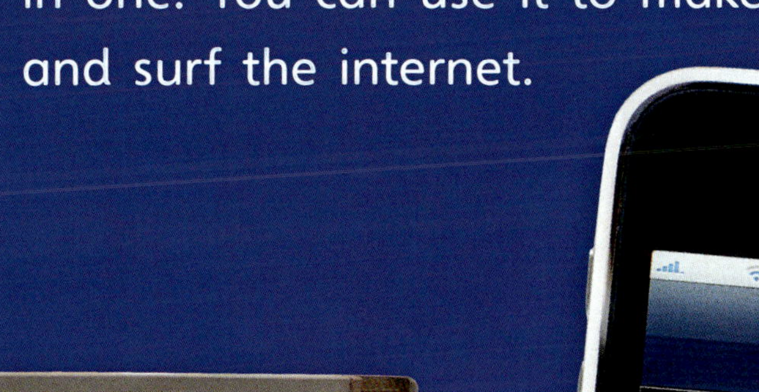

Excellent Gadgets

Today, almost every **gadget** we use has a tiny "engine" in it. This tiny engine is called a **microprocessor**.

Microprocessors are found in excellent gadgets such as cameras and televisions. They are even found in planes and cars.

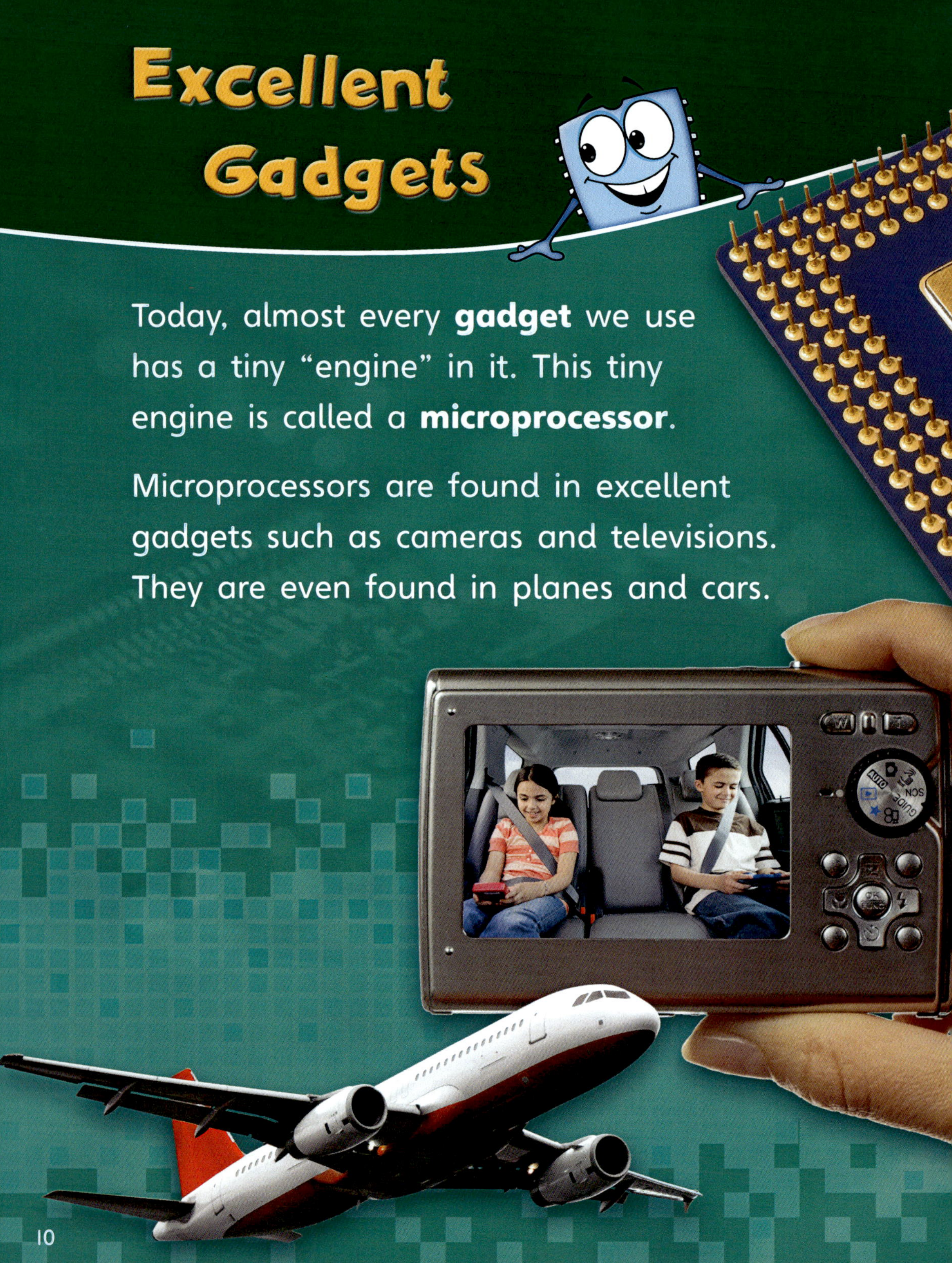

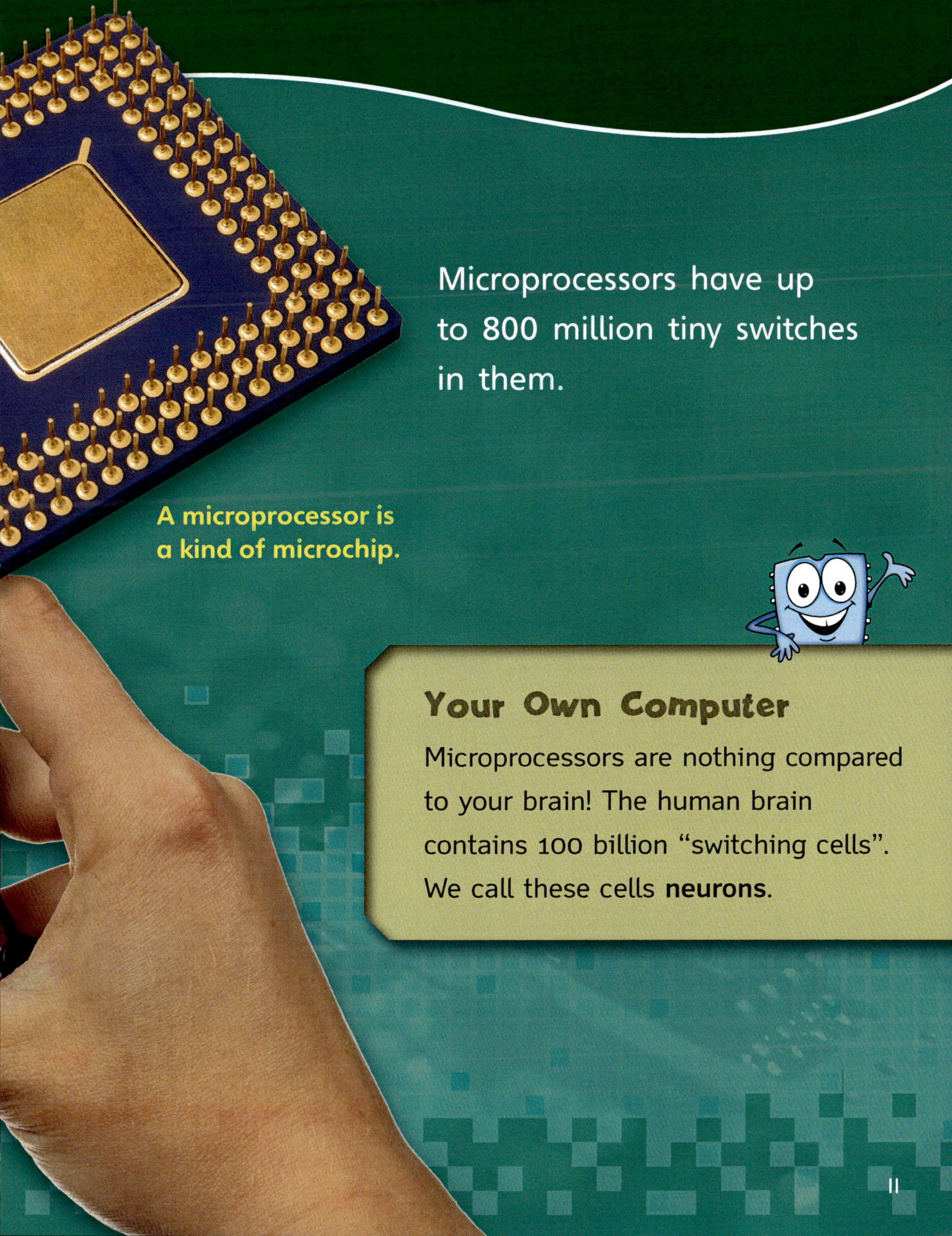

Microprocessors have up to 800 million tiny switches in them.

A microprocessor is a kind of microchip.

Your Own Computer

Microprocessors are nothing compared to your brain! The human brain contains 100 billion "switching cells". We call these cells **neurons**.

Let's Play

Follow me and meet some of my friends. They're excellent gadgets, too!

A New Way to Game – Wii

Video games used to be played sitting down. Now, games such as Nintendo Wii™ can make you sweat!

It's all thanks to Wii's controller. The controller senses the way a player moves. The controller can be used as all sorts of things, such as a fishing rod, golf club or steering wheel.

In the Palm of Your Hand

This is a Nintendo GAME BOY™. It was invented in 1989. It was one of the first video games small enough to hold in your hands.

Now check this out! It's a Nintendo DS™ Lite. It has two screens and 3D graphics. Wow!

SpaceWar!

These white dots don't look like much, but they were the start of computer games. The game SpaceWar! is nearly 50 years old!

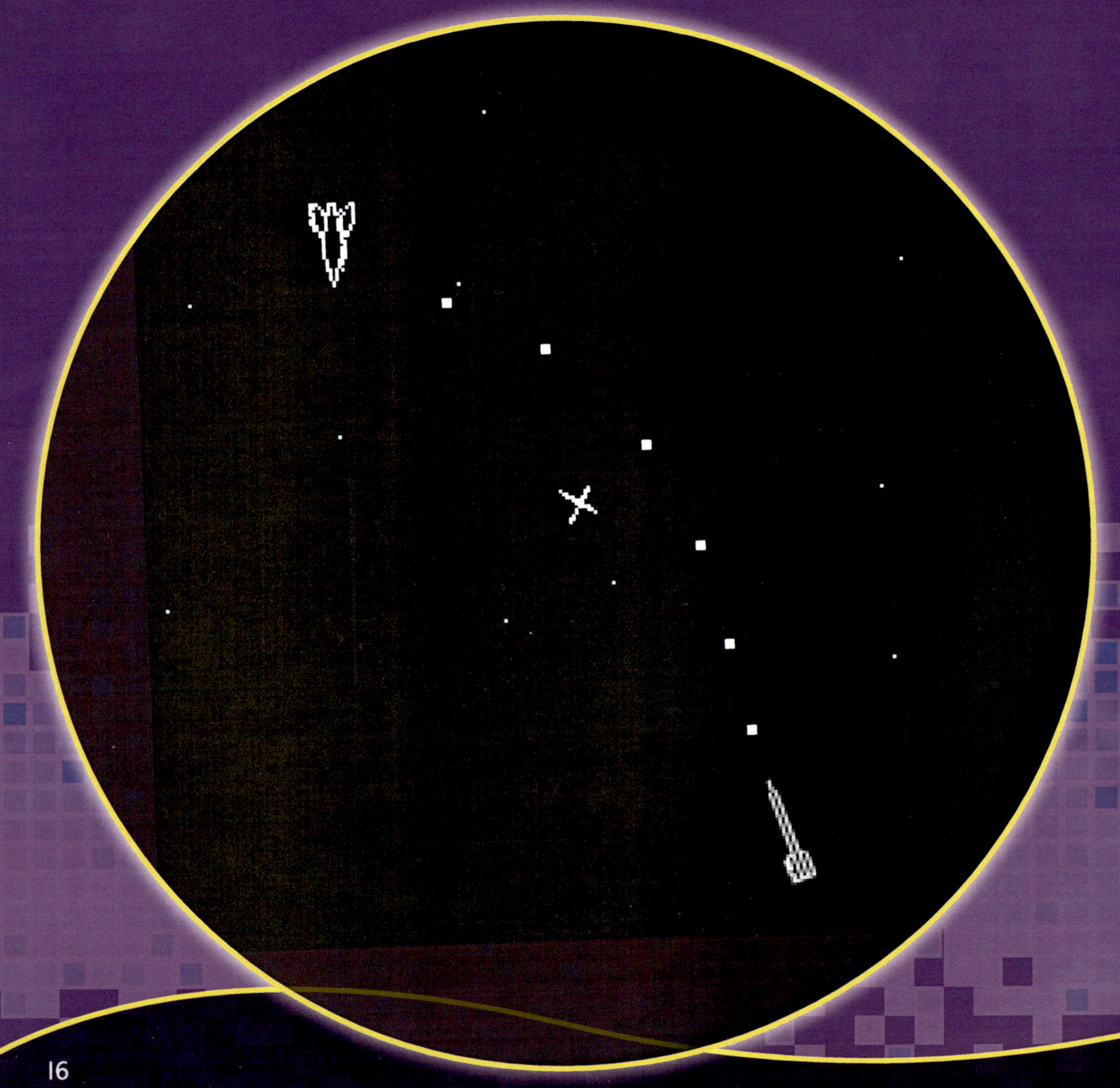

Space Invaders

An early video game that came out in 1978 was Space Invaders. It was played on a big machine. You put money in the machine to play the game.

Space Invaders is one of the most popular games in history.

Are Books Ancient History?

Books are a big part of our lives today. In a hundred years, the book as we know it may not be part of people's lives at all. People might be reading e-books.

Kindle

The Kindle lets you **download** books. You then read them on a small screen. Kindle is the same size as a chapter book and uses "electronic paper"! You turn the pages by pressing buttons.

Digital Library

You can also read old and **rare** books on the internet. One library has put some of its rare books on a special website. You go to that website and read the books!

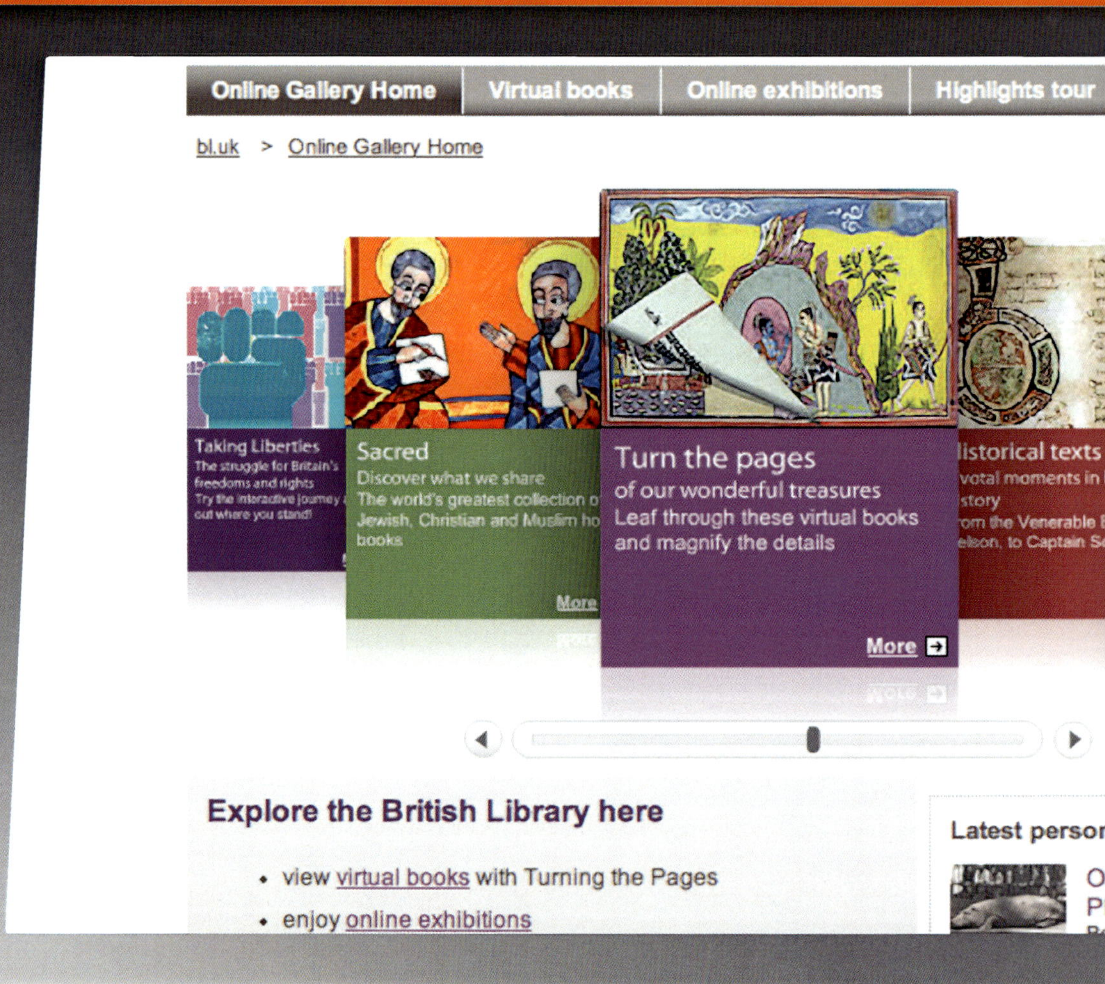

This picture is from a very, very old book kept in a library. You can see pages of the book on the internet.

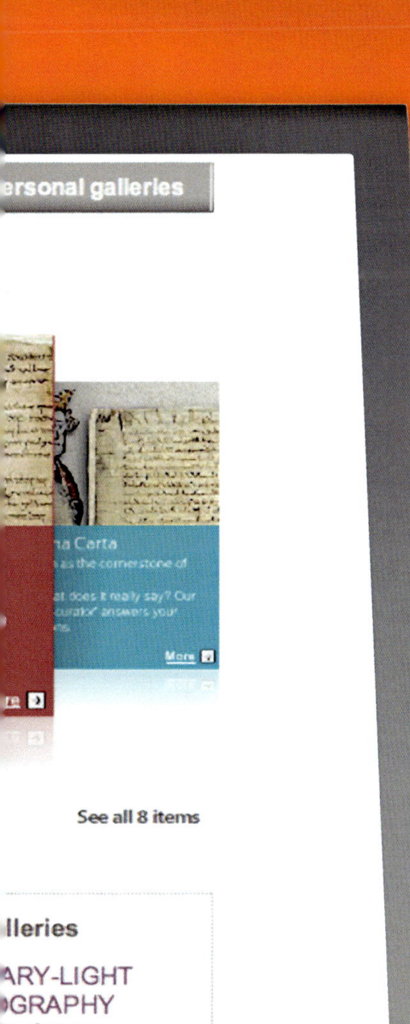

Music Anywhere

The Sony Walkman was the first pocket-sized music player. It played cassette tapes! It is much bigger than today's music players.

The iPod plays digital music files. But it also stores photos, games and movies. Many iPods also have a camera in them, too!

Did You Know?

The first song ever recorded was *Mary Had a Little Lamb*. It was played on a machine called a **phonograph**.

Call Me!

Today, many people have a mobile phone. Mobile phones weren't always the small gadgets we know today. They used to be the size and weight of a house brick. Imagine carrying that in your pocket!

This early mobile phone had a handset linked to a heavy case. The case was filled mostly with batteries.

This is what mobile phones looked like when they were first invented.

Is There Anything They Can't Do?

Today, mobiles aren't just phones. Many people use their mobiles to surf the internet, listen to music and play games.

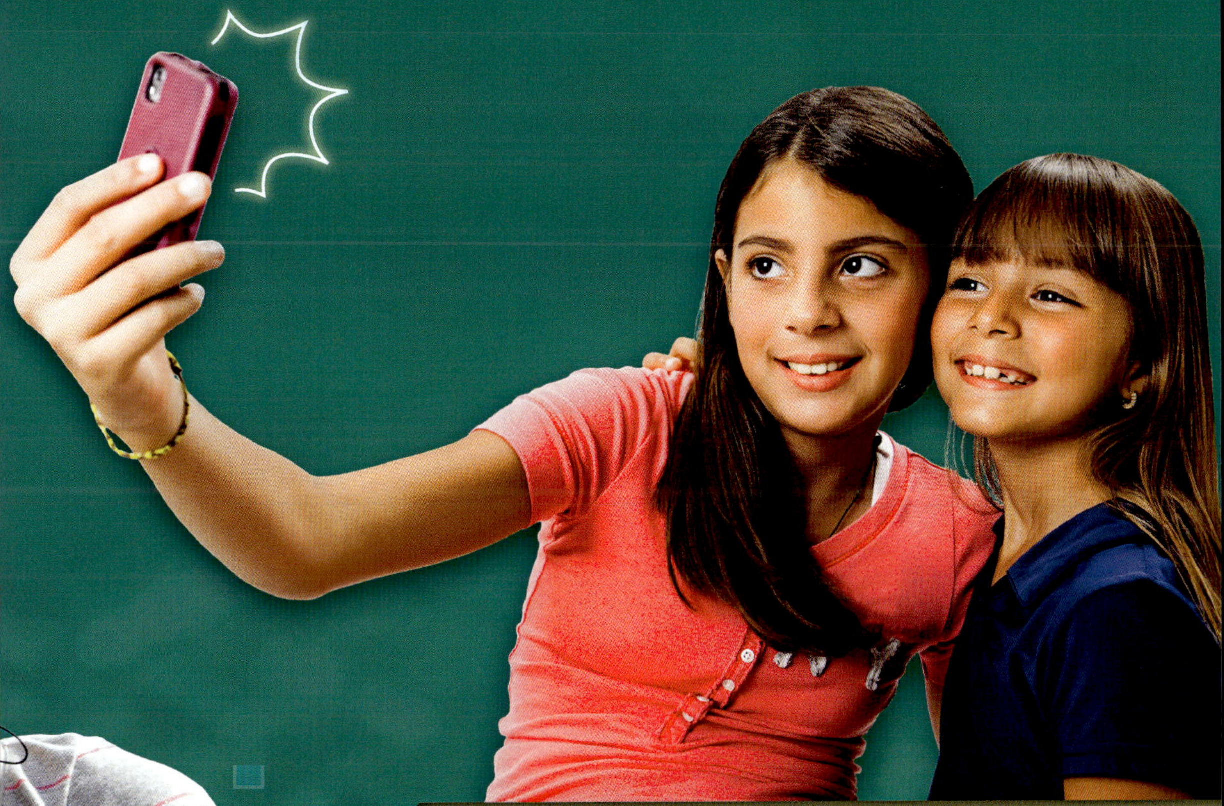

Did You Know?

Old mobile phones are a big threat to our environment. They can take more than 500 years to break down. Make sure your old phones are recycled.

Into the Future

Technology changes almost every day. My friends and I will keep changing in exciting ways. Some of us will get bigger. Most of us will probably get smaller!

What do you think technology will be like in 20 years?

Excellent Gadget Timeline

3000 BC Abacus first used

1822 Charles Babbage tries to build an adding up machine

1877 First song recorded on a phonograph

1946 ENIAC, the first electronic computer, is built

1962 SpaceWar! is released

1977 Apple II computer is released

1979 Sony Walkman is released

1989 Nintendo GAME BOY™ is released

2001 iPod is released

2006 Nintendo Wii™ is released

2007 Kindle is released

Glossary

computers	machines that receive, store and give out information
download	to copy information from one computer to another, or from the internet
electrical circuits	gadgets that electrical currents flow through
gadget	an object that is used to do something fun
invented	made for the first time
microchip	a small gadget that helps computers to run and to remember information
microprocessor	the computer "engine"; a type of microchip
neurons	nerve cells that carry messages within the body
personal	belonging to a person
phonograph	a music player and recorder that was used from the 1870s through the 1980s. It's a bit like a record player.
rare	not found very often
technology	gadgets, such as machines, that help us do things quicker and faster
transistors	tiny switches that work together to help computers do calculations

Index